MENENIUS The augurer tells me we shall have news to-night *Coriolanus, Act II*

AN EXPERIENCE OF CRITICS

THE DRAMATIC CRITIC: Legend and Reality

CHRISTOPHER FRY

AN EXPERIENCE OF CRITICS

and THE APPROACH TO DRAMATIC CRITICISM by
Ivor Brown, W. A. Darlington, Alan Dent, Harold Hobson,
Philip Hope-Wallace, Eric Keown, J. C. Trewin, T. C. Worsley
Edited by Kaye Webb

With a prologue by
ALEC GUINNESS

Drawings by
RONALD SEARLE

New York
OXFORD UNIVERSITY PRESS
1953

The drawings on pages 33 and 59 are reproduced by
permission of the proprietors of Punch

CONTENTS

5

PROLOGUE by ALEC GUINNESS

To ask an actor to write a few words, by way of preface, on dramatic critics is like asking oil to make a comment on vinegar. I must hasten to add that you will find very little vinegar in this charming book. You will find, on the contrary, such charity, such affability and good sense that naturally you will ask yourself, "Why? How has this come about?"— until it has dawned on you that the critics are writing about themselves and their art. You will find precious few references to actors or contemporary playwrights.

There are three ways, I suggest, for a determined actor to deal with critics. The first, most sensational, slightly dangerous but highly successful if carried out with sincerity, is to hit them. This has been proved in our time by a fine actor pushing very hard with his fist at a critic's shoulder. It wasn't exactly a punch—just a not-too-friendly gesture—but it resulted in a series of lovely notices which enabled the actor to advance to acknowledged greatness. The second method is for the actor to pretend he doesn't read what the critics write. I don't recommend this, as I fear it no longer carries conviction. The third way, and far the most fatiguing, is for the actor to arm himself with scissors and paste, carefully cut out the relevant critical columns and preserve them in a huge commonplace-book. These can always be read in jaded moments (for it is rare for an actor to cling to adverse criticisms) and quite soon they acquire a yellowish-grey faded colour which puts the whole thing in *perspective. If the actor is of a philosophical turn, he will argue that the critics' statements cancel each other out and consequently don't exist. Critics are seldom unanimous, which is one of the most endearing things about them.*

My favourite cancelling out occurred when I was playing Richard II for the Old Vic. One reputable critic said I had no music in my verse-speaking, while another said it was like listening to Bach. Not everyone has a taste for Bach, of course.

Does an actor change a performance after reading criticism? Probably more often than critics, who usually only see one performance, realise, though it is a difficult thing to do. I have modified consciously two performances, realising that what a critic had written was just, imaginative and helpful and that alteration wouldn't interfere greatly with my fellow players (though I fear I have never shaved on critical advice, whatever the gossip columnists may say). On the other hand, I would never think of tackling a classical role without at some time browsing through Coleridge, Lamb, Hazlitt, Montague, Lewes and Shaw in the hope, if not of inspiration, then at least of stimulation. Actors read too much, which is our compliment to the critics.

Dramatic criticism, it seems to me, requires two things of paramount importance: (a) readability—which rules out French, Latin, German, tiresome quotations, puns, etc.; and (b) the gift of conjuring up for the reader a visual picture of a performance. The late James Agate was a great critic because, although there were sometimes lumps of Racine in his column, he managed in a neat, clean phrase to show you the essential characteristic of an actor's work and often its profundity. He always re-created for the reader the vitality he had found in the theatre, and if the performance or play was dull, his journalism remained superb and his love of the theatre constant. I don't think anyone who also loves the theatre can ask for more than that; it is worth all the championing of the unities, and infinitely more than the indulgent patronage to which playwrights and actors are sometimes subjected. Hard criticism never hurts. (Mr. Cuthbert Worsley must be very out of touch with the professional theatre if he really thinks plays are put on by mutual admiration societies.) What hurts is viciousness, mercifully rare in our Press, and what wounds, making the actor feel a shabby charlatan, is glowing praise for what he knows is indifferent work. (This includes, of course, praise for other actors' worthless performances as well as his own!) When all is said and done, actors feel they know as much about acting, if not more, than anyone else; which does not mean that they wish to deny the professional connoisseur his place in the theatre.

This little book, admirably put together, is an attempt to clarify that place in the theatre; I hope you will find it as stimulating as I did. Mr. Christopher Fry starts the ball rolling with a fine spin.

To express my own goodwill, in case this preface has not been taken as lightheartedly as intended, I wish the critics more space in the future, and carte blanche *to Mr. Ronald Searle.*

London, July 1952

PART ONE

AN EXPERIENCE OF CRITICS

CHRISTOPHER FRY

I feel like a Fourth-form boy who has been invited up to the masters' common-room to comment on the year's teaching: somewhat overwhelmed by the privilege, somewhat emboldened by the nudgings of my schoolmates and their last urgent whispers of "Go on; you tell them, Fry", and, as a precautionary measure, copies of all the newspapers folded into the seat of my trousers, the dramatic criticism outwards.

I don't know how I can help feeling like this, for to some extent this is what the relationship has become between critic and artist or whatever word will serve to cover actor, playwright, producer and designer. The masters write their reports: "Could do better if he tried", or "Seems to make no effort to be intelligible", or "Has ability, but should try to concentrate on the matter in hand"; and the boys draw irreverent caricatures in the margins of their manuscripts. It isn't a very rewarding relationship; neither is it one which is unavoidable, but it has come about, and it would be good if we could discover why.

The simplest explanation is that, on the one hand, no man's judgment is infallible; and, on the other, that an artist thinks well only of a critic who thinks well of *him*; and, I admit, it is interesting to hear the writer say to the painter, or the film-director say to the theatre-producer, "Of course, your critics aren't so bad, but *ours* are terrible", and the cry of anguished protest that comes in reply.

So simple an explanation, however, accounts for no more than the moments of disappointment or injured vanity. No man in his senses expects a critic always to be right—indeed, it would be very disconcerting if he were: we should have to believe him, and the knowledge of his fallibility is often a great comfort. The simple explanation also falls short on another point: the artist, at some level of himself, will respect an adverse criticism, if he can understand it; he has no wish to get away with anything, and he is so close to his work that he is, or should be, glad of a more distant eye.

But he must also be allowed a certain arrogance: a degree of carefree confidence, if his work is not to be in some way blunted. Whatever medium he works in, words, or paint, or notation, will see to it that he is never far from humility. He knows before he starts that he is attempting the impossible; he knows that existence cannot be demonstrated, or even adequately commented upon, except by existence; and he would sometimes prefer to be doing something comparatively easy, such as cleaning the Augean stables, or, as he may think in his less amiable moments, such as being a critic.

An artist's sensitiveness to criticism is, at least in part, an effort to keep unimpaired the zest, or confidence, or arrogance, which he needs to make creation possible; or an instinct to climb through

He is never far from humility

his problems in his own way as he should, and must; and it isn't surprising to look back to Hardy putting down his novelist's pen after the reception of *Jude the Obscure*; or to Tennyson walking the Downs and saying over and over again, "He says I'm not a great poet; he says I'm not a great poet".

He may not have been a great poet, but he was a good one, and might, I think, have been even better if the critics had been as creative in their way as he was in his. But creative criticism—by which I mean criticism that takes as its starting-place the individual talent it deals with, and not some ready rule of thumb or personal preference—creative criticism has always been rare, and continues so, and much of the rest, though plentiful, is as boring as a small child who insists on being looked at. And everywhere to-day can be heard the patter of tiny criticism, the busy sound of men continually knowing what they like. How anything manages to create itself at all is a wonder. The newly sprouting acorn is dug up several times a week, and solemnly told that, whatever it may think to the contrary, it is not an oak-tree. It must understand that it is nothing more nor less than an acorn being pretentious.

I am not, you will have noticed, yet talking particularly of dramatic criticism. That is a grave thought towards which I am feeling my way sentence by sentence; for if I think that dramatic criticism is not all that it should be, it is because I think that no criticism is all that it should be. And artists themselves are often the worst offenders. One might think that a man who knows, by his own experience, how difficult it is to convey anything to anybody, even to himself, would be patient and forgiving to his fellows, however clumsily they flounder forward; but the history of literary feuds is long; and it is no uncommon thing to find one writer attacking another, ignoring what strength, or promise of strength, there may be for the pleasure of declaring the weakness.

Whereas he should know to fall on his knees and cry, "This man has written a sentence : he has actually written a sentence !"—or, if that should be an overestimation, he might say: "Look, look; here are two words which have come together in God."

That is the only true method of criticism between artists. But critics may reasonably feel that something further is expected of them. Dramatic critics, for example, may hesitate to say, "No one who loves the theatre should fail to pay fifteen shillings for a stall at the Globe where, in the second act of Mr. Fry's new play, he may hear several minutes of dialogue which is not entirely inapt".

Something further is expected of them; and something so difficult that I wonder if there is a pin to choose between the ardours of creating and criticising.

A fine dramatic critic of the future is already
with us. He paid, not long ago, his first visit to the
theatre. He sat in the front of a box, with five years'
experience of the world behind him, and watched
a pantomime. His eyes never left the stage; even
through the intervals he refused to be distracted
by ice-cream or lemonade; he stared at the curtain, waiting for it to go up again. Neither the
Dame, nor the comedy horse, nor the Broker's
men, nor the Dagenham Girl Pipers could win a
smile from him. He remained, expressionless and
absorbed, the representation of the perfect critic.
At the Transformation Scene he turned to his
father, and made his only comment. He said:
"Well, we didn't expect that, did we?"

I take up your time with this story because it may
be that, on our first visit to the theatre, we are innocent of everything except sensibility; there is no
confusion: we know when we are touched; and
this is a good condition for criticism. I don't mean
that a critic must abandon all thought of ice-cream
or lemonade in the interval, but ideally there
should be nothing, no preconception of what a play
is, no impatience, no demands, between him and
the stage; only a readiness to receive.

I do not know how it is to be done, and of all
places at a first night. A first-night audience is as
though a very large family had suddenly been re-
united in the bronchial ward of a hospital. And the

Abandon all thoughts of ice-cream or lemonade in the interval

critic must reach across this uneasy state of affairs, and be in perfect communion with the complexities of play, players and production. Upon his judgment depend the livelihood and career of nerve-jangled men and women who have been working at high pressure for several weeks. He must have a subtle understanding of playwriting, acting and production, so that a fault shall not be laid at the wrong door: a misjudgment which happens in criticism often enough to be a major problem. He must have the patience and concentration of a bird-watcher, the eye of a sleuth, the capacity for experience of an explorer . . . but all this you are already gravely aware of; and I want you to know, before I take the next step, that I wouldn't undertake a profession so full of complications and pitfalls if you paid me; and if, in this talk, I am only a fault-finder, it is not because I can see no good in critics, for I do; and I know how willing many of them are to turn and say, "Well, we didn't expect that, did we?"; it is because I should like to trace, if I can, those things which divide us in understanding.

There have been two occasions when I have been somewhat in the position of critic: once when I had promised to write about a production for a theatrical magazine, and I could scarcely hear a word of the play for the noise of my own mind wondering how I should write about it; and again, when I was one of the judges of a play competition organised by the Arts Theatre. The result of that was the first night of a play called *Saints' Day*: and the result of *that* was as though the ground between critics and non-critics had suddenly split open to the depth of several letters to *The Times* and the *Telegraph*.

It seemed as though the play contained all, or most, of the differences between those who are in the theatre and those who sit in judgment upon it. Almost I would say it *was* the difference; and for that reason I make no apology for returning to it. The critics condemned the play very nearly unanimously. Actors, producers, writers—apparently just as unanimously—felt it to move in the theatre like the stirring of a new power. What could such a complete division mean?

There have been occasions when I have felt that a play of quality has been killed by the Press (*Skipper Next to God* at the Embassy in 1945 or 1946 was an example of this); but I had never before been driven to think that the whole critical profession had chosen to look out of only one eye. The purpose of a play-competition at an Arts Theatre is not, primarily, to discover a commercial success, though we should all have been delighted if one had turned up, but to find an original talent which should be encouraged and given the opportunity to grow. This was what, by good fortune, we found: characters which the actors delighted in playing;

very often a dramatic economy which presented in
a few bare lines' what would take many dramatists
half an act; a sense conveyed of a haunted world,
haunted by human beings unable to understand
themselves or each other, haunted by fear of life,
by the wooing of the powers of death, haunted by
will-lessness and lack of love.

Also the play was most professionally shaped. I
am often puzzled by what a critic will call good construction: an act of a play, for example, in which a
succession of two-handed scenes follow one another
like sister-acts in a music-hall. It is part of a play's
construction that the action should be dispensed by
characters meeting in a pattern and variation of
numbers; and the pattern and the theatre-sense
of the first two acts of *Saints' Day* seemed to many
of us unmistakable.

Then comes the question of the play's obscurity,
and there is no question: it is obscure. It is obscure, that is to say, to the brain. It is not, I think,
at all obscure to the nerves. It is obscure if we
must always know where we are. It is not obscure
if we think it good sometimes to ask, "Where are
we?" It is obscure and not obscure as a man's self is
obscure and not obscure. It is when the characters
seemed about to address themselves to our brains,
or when we seemed to come up against a devised
symbolism, that the play became untrue to itself.

There were indications here and there among the

Where are we?

critics that, even though we so strongly disagreed with them, we should not have said so: it was all very well to give the play the prize, but we shouldn't have insisted that it was good; and only a few days ago I saw an echo of this in the Press, which seemed to say that if actors, producers and playwrights join in asserting that an injustice has been done, they are to be laughed off as being soft-hearted, uncritical, hand-in-glove, incapable, in fact, of judging quality in the profession they practise, or else deliberately deceiving themselves and everybody else.

I suggest that if it is possible for the artists to learn from the critics (and I think it is), then it shouldn't be altogether improbable that the critics could sometimes learn from the artists. The history of criticism through the centuries isn't one unbroken progress of accurate judgment; and I don't know why critics, like Victorian parents, should be disturbed by admitting to their children that they also make mistakes. There is no progress that way. It's a hardening of the arteries of understanding. A man's work is what his life is; and he can only grow where he seeks.

Sometimes when I am trying to work I think of the picture of myself which emerges from the press-cuttings, and it seems, in a way, very splendid. I see a man reeling intoxicated with words; they flow in a golden—or perhaps pinchbeck—stream from his mouth: they start out at his ears; they burst like rockets and jumping crackers and catherine-wheels round his head; they spring in wanton sport at his feet and trip him; but trip him or not, he loves them: let them all come, go where they may; let them strangle sense, flood the stage, break the dams of form: facility shall have its day. His typewriter continues to chatter long after it has been put back in its case. Words will grow out of him, like finger-nails, for some time after his death.

Then, having looked at this picture and marvelled, I turn back to my typewriter. Like an ancient Red Indian chief, I sit for some hours in silence. At last I am ready to speak, and say "How", or perhaps some slightly longer word. My two fingers withdraw from the typewriter and the night wears dumbly on towards dawn.

The Lady's not for Burning, the play which first gave rise to the bacchic figure vomiting his careless words, was five or six months finding its shape before writing began, and eight months in writing. I don't mean that slowness in writing is a virtue: it is an incapacity; but it's hard to relate it to verbal intoxication; it feels more like a slow death by ground glass.

What do I think I'm doing, then, so painfully creating a false impression? Why so many words? Why so many apparent interruptions of the relevant action of the play? There is no doubt that, looked at from many points of view, these are most reasonable questions to ask; and I can only try to explain what was in my mind.

So many words, for instance. We know this criticism doesn't precisely mean what it says. There are the same number of words as in any other play; you have only to count them. It means, I think, that I don't use the same words often enough; or else, or as well, that the words are an ornament on the meaning and not the meaning itself. That is certainly sometimes—perhaps often—true in the comedies, though almost as often I have meant the ornament to be, dramatically or comedically, an essential part of the meaning; and in my more sanguine moments I think the words are as exact to my purpose as I could make them at the time of writing.

And then the question of relevance. The question is, relevance to what? The relevance of one kind of play is not necessarily the relevance of another: I tried to say so in *The Lady* in the line: "*That same laughter, madam, is an irrelevance that almost amounts to revelation*", and I think what I am most anxious to

Words are an ornament on the meaning

do here is to ask that criticism should look more
deeply into the nature of a play, and to pursue
the reason for its nature, rather than to try to
force it into a category to which it doesn't belong.
If a criticism is to be understood and profited
by, writer and critic must start with the same
premiss.

Comedy is not a drama with the addition of
laughs. It is a world of its own, and when we leave
it again, it can have given to the world of action we
rejoin something of a new cast. It is a world of its
own, but not a world all of one kind—it may be of
situation; or the sunny, tensionless world of *As You
Like It* where, for all Jacques' talk of time, there is
all the time in the world; or a world of wit, such
as *The Way of the World*, where plot is an infernal
nuisance, so huddled together to be out of the way
of the true comedy that it took me hours to work
it out before I produced it at Oxford; and after a
few days of rehearsal I could no longer explain it to
any member of the cast who thought perhaps he
should know what the story was about.

As comedy is not a drama with laughs, so a verse
play is not a prose play which happens to be written in verse. It has its own nature. In a talk on
Poetry and the Theatre I tried saying something more
about this, in these words: "The dramatist must
view the world of his play, and the people of that
world, with great precision: the poet-dramatist

with the greatest poetic precision. The whole struc-
ture depends upon it, what scene follows another,
what character goes and what character enters,
where description or landscape becomes part of the
action, or where it needs a bare exchange. The
poetry and the construction are inseparate. Who
understands the poetry understands the construction, who understands the construction understands the poetry, for the poetry is the action, and
the action—even apart from the words—is the
figure of the poetry. . . ."—I do not mean that my
own plays live up to this definition; but this is the
ground upon which, now and in the future, I must
meet the critics.

If this all seems to be turning into a defence of
Fry, it is not at all what I mean by it. For every
point I raise there are half a dozen more which, in
the circumstances, I don't intend to refer to, pre-
ferring to withhold, as far as possible, the stick
which you could beat me with. But it is a fairly
general experience of writers, producers, actors,
to find themselves being judged from some altogether other part of the forest, where the critic has
dug himself in as though for a siege; and I can best
show the kind of misunderstanding I mean by in-
stances from my own experience.

There are many orders of such misunderstanding.
There is the criticism which seems wantonly to
misrepresent, so that it can make a point; as when,

for instance, a well-known critic (not in this country), to prove that I sometimes wrote pretentious nonsense, quoted a line which was not in the play at all!

Or there is the kind of criticism which seems anxious to pick a hole at all costs: such as that which soundly berated an artificial comedy for having no lines in it as simple and highly charged as those in *King Lear*. Or this: in *Venus Observed* the Duke ends a speech with, "And I, as unlaborious as a laburnum tree, hang in caresses of gold", and the critic then comments, "An inaccurate observation, since a laburnum is only apparently 'unlaborious' ". I see what he means: like the only apparently untoiling and unspinning lilies of the field. These are small matters, but they show the larger fault: that sometimes a critic will rather cavil at the surface than give judgment in depth.

A few paragraphs ago I mentioned the word "pretentious". I will state my belief that it is not a critical word. It usually means that, in the critic's opinion, a man's reach has exceeded his grasp, and what hope is there for the theatre without such temeritous reaching? There may be times when we lay ourselves open to it by an insincerity, but even so, it is a dangerously facile word, and too easily covers up a critic's impatience.

A critic rightly expects that those he criticises should go as far as their powers will take them in

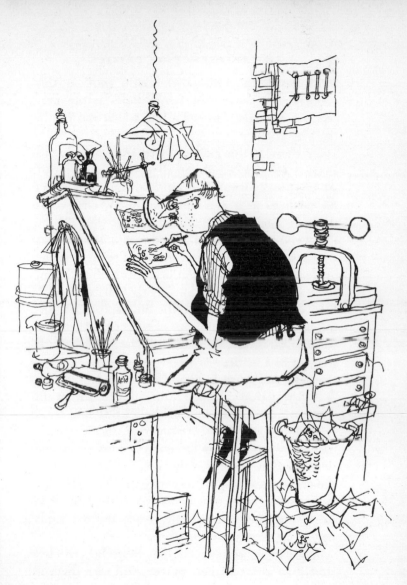

In whatever art they practise . . .

whatever art they practise: they should be honest, devoted, sensitive, laborious to perfect what they do, never content to rest on what they have done, but ever restless to increase the scope of what is still to follow. Are they not to expect as much from their critics? But, round and about those who know the gravity of their work, are others whose ability is to make rapid decisions about everything and everybody; and the less they are inclined to consider the greater is their air of omniscience.

They do not belong, evidently, to a recent race of beings. John Gay, in the *Rehearsal at Goatham*, says, "They can scarce be called critics who must hear and read a thing before they will venture to declare their opinion. Anybody can do that". And, though I have no doubt that they now in fact attend what they criticise, it is equally sure that they do not take in what they criticise or would even know how to set about it; and, to make up for this apparently unimportant deficiency, their power of scorn is tremendous.

I could give you examples of the games they play, but it is better to move on to something of a more interesting sort; and I must ask your forbearance while once more, and for the last time, I bring my own work in as an example. In this instance it concerns critic and playwright, but, in its kind, it might equally be true of critic and actor, or critic and producer—an example of their not being in accord, and yet the critic serving as that outward eye which can be of such value. Sometimes when we say the critic is wrong, we might do well to ask what, in ourselves, led him to be wrong.

There is a climax in my play *The Firstborn* which several critics whose opinion I respect found to be insufficiently prepared. It was the moment when Moses suddenly understands that the last plague of Egypt, the Death of the Firstborn, means the death of his nephew-by-adoption, Rameses. The critics felt, very reasonably, that the affection between Moses and Rameses had been so barely touched on that three-quarters of the impact of Moses' realisation was lost.

Now I had not imagined any such personal affection on the part of Moses. In the play he meets Rameses for a bare five minutes: is touched by his hero-worship: recognises the boy's sincerity and humanity, and that is all. What I hoped I had shown, and hadn't, was that to Moses the boy represented Moses' own boyhood when he was Prince of Egypt, represented also that love for Egypt which Moses couldn't shake off even while he was fighting her. There are certainly speeches to that effect, and Moses, in the moment of realisation, cries, "Egypt, Egypt! He was meant for Egypt!"; but the speeches were not enough: I had, in this instance, led the critic to be wrong; and since the writing of *The Firstborn* I have been learning too reluctantly that neither audiences nor critics are clairvoyant.

I hope to mend my ways. We are all, I think, anxious to mend our ways, once we can see clearly where and how they should be mended. But we cannot trust the critic to tell us unless he *also* knows moments of prayer and fasting and self-distrust; unless he judges, not by a jaunty reflex-action, but by drawing into himself what he judges before giving judgment; unless we can be sure that he gets no pleasure from wounding, or belittles others to give himself the appearance of size; and that he has always before him, like a fearful warning, those evasions, dishonesties and tricks protective of self-esteem, which are the badges of the little critic who knows what he likes but will never know anything more. I made a character in a play describe justice as the crossing of mind with mind; and I believe this to be true of just and creative criticism.

"An Experience of Critics" was first delivered as an address to the Critics' Circle on April 28, 1952, at The Arts Theatre, London

PART TWO

THE APPROACH TO
DRAMATIC CRITICISM

a symposium

IVOR BROWN

I AM ASKED for my Approach to Dramatic Criticism. It is, I must confess, through the Stalls Entrance. I am well aware that theatre critics ought to be placed further off, higher up, and even in the back row of the gallery. But shall I say that I have a bad head for heights and that Miss Katharine Hepburn can make one giddy at any range? Or shall I honestly confess that the flesh is unwilling and that I like my comfort? In any case, the managers are not going to reserve the roof for our tribe. They have quite enough trouble with it, anyway.

I make the Approach because I have liked and still like the theatre (most of the time) and would have ceased approaching it long ago if I had not liked it. No critic has any right to his place of privilege (and to his salary) if he has become bored with the art in question. Critics must be "stage-struck" folk. Weariness is unforgivable. Those whom the drama has turned queasy should quit.

I believe that the ideal critic is an enthusiastic introducer. True, he must dismiss the shoddy as such. But his primary function is not to go slamming about the place and showing what a bright boy he is, but to act as a persuasive, not a dictatorial, guide. He can dismiss his dislikes briefly; his admirations he should communicate as fully as possible in these days of scanty space.

The public is too docile, especially, I am told, in New York, where two or three men are said to be the dictators of box-office success. This is a shocking state of affairs and I hope it will not get as bad as that over here. I trust that any who read my notices will go their own way and be courageously selective. My negatives should not be theirs. The critic is read, I take it, for his personal response to a performance and for any grace of style or wit that he can display in making it. His views are individual, fallible, and not to be followed mechanically.

It is the primary business of a critic to be readable. He owes that to his editor, to the buyers of the paper, and above all to the artists. What is the use of powerful approbation if nobody can wade through it? The theatre is not helped by chunks of what is known in some newspaper offices as "basic slag".

On the other hand, the effort to be readable should not involve cheap scores at the author's or artist's expense. It is easy to approach a play with a sour quip on its title and a few other ready-made jokes. Nor do I favour cutting remarks, even though justified, about the personal appearance of the players That a player is too old or insufficiently handsome for a part can be sufficiently intimated without having to lacerate the feelings of the artist. The public may titter over some "crack" of this kind, but it is a poor way of being readable. The critic can be mannerly without being misleading. He ought to know and love the history of the theatre if he is to serve its present and promote its future. Above all, he ought to realise that a single sentence may do cruel harm to a number of people, in self-respect as well as in finance and employment. This is not to say that he should never censure; but his damns must follow deliberation and his curses be tempered by courtesy.

IVOR BROWN

W. A. DARLINGTON

PEOPLE SEEM to be very sorry for dramatic critics on daily papers. I spend quite a lot of my time being commiserated with by actors, by readers, by personal acquaintances, even by my colleagues who write for the weekly papers, on the impossible conditions in which my work is done. This article seems to give me a good chance to make it plain that neither I nor any other experienced daily-paper critic considers himself a proper object for pity. We like our impossible conditions. We like writing immediately after curtain-fall, before the excitement of the first night has had time to cool, and with the stimulating knowledge that the printing-presses are waiting for us down below.

Doubtless we write a little less well than we might. Doubtless, given leisure, we could select our adjectives or turn our phrases more effectively; though we like to believe that we make up in urgency and warmth for what we lack in verbal precision and grace. But on the point of our actual writing, comment is generous. People realise that the ability to write quickly is a professional skill developed by long practice, and are on the whole impressed by it. What they pity us for is the necessity to make up our minds quickly. "How can he give a considered judgment if he has to dash away to Fleet Street and scribble the instant the curtain is down?" That is the usual form of the question; and it seems to me to show a blank ignorance of how the critic's mind works.

Almost always, the "opinion" which a critic is called upon to express is not a reasoned judgment alterable by argument.

W. A. DARLINGTON

It is a report on an emotional reaction subconsciously experienced during the action of the play, and is not susceptible to argument at all. The daily-paper critic acquires a knack of getting swiftly in touch with his subconscious mind, and knows his opinion at, or very shortly after, the end of the play. (A. B. Walkley used to say that when the play ended he never knew what he thought of it, but by the time he reached Printing House Square he always knew precisely.)

An example: A few years back a very good actor played Hamlet very well. The character was intelligently rendered, the poetry finely delivered. I followed the performance with admiration and at the end I turned, so to speak, to my subconscious and said, "Well?" Its reply was instantaneous and firm, "I have not once been emotionally stirred". My notice lay clear before me. Admiration for professional accomplishment; regret that accomplishment was not enough.

I can prove in my own person that the daily-paper critic, given the chance, would hardly ever go back on his first-night verdict. I get the chance regularly once a month, when I write an article on the London Theatre for the *New York Times*. Here is the ideal opportunity for second thoughts, for even if changing one's mind were a crime, nobody would be likely to catch me at it, 3000 miles away. Yet in fourteen years I have never altered my original opinion.

Desmond MacCarthy once said, "I let the play wash over me, and then examine the markings in the sand". That phrase hits off very happily the main facts; that the critic does not become a critic until the play is over, that his mind works backwards, and that his first need is to teach his subconscious its job.

ALAN DENT

Pace PRACTICALLY EVERYBODY, there seems to me to be nothing very much wrong with dramatic criticism. Some of us write in too many papers, some of us write in too few, and none of us writes half as well—nowadays—as the great line which began with Leigh Hunt and concluded with the death of Agate.

But the general level is not despicable—it is just fairly low or fairish. Space restriction—from which the daily-paper critics suffer very much more than the weekly ones—has done one valuable thing : it has gagged and manacled the bores. There is nowadays too little space, admittedly. But in the old days there was too much, and even the good critics, with rather too much space to fill instead of too little, became victims of the writer's occupational diseases of redundance and tautology. (If any reader questions this statement, let him peruse a sheaf of current American notices of any new play on Broadway— always provided, of course, that he has six hours of leisure to spare.)

The state of our criticism—I say again—could be better, but it could also be much worse. Our manners—with a few juvenile exceptions—are distinctly better than they used to be. Our culture is terrific (even three-ha'penny papers quote Kafka and Kierkegaard). Our lack of reverence for past glories is worthy of the youngest undergraduates at the oldest universities. Our style may be clipped, but it remains (we think) caustic. Our wit may lack the trenchancy of Shaw, the subtlety of Beerbohm, or the urbanity of Walkley, but we may, not without justice, claim for it that at least it has pep and zip! We are no wasters of words, because we have no space to waste them in. We may not be Hazlitts, nowadays, nor C. E. Montagues; but we believe that we still contrive to be, in our own not too small and not too modest way, "swell".

Although invited to be personal in this statement about the state of dramatic criticism, I prefer to keep my own personality out of it, preserving this for my own criticism (where it belongs, if it belongs anywhere). The truth is—and it is a truth I have long had at the back of my mind—that there are three distinct varieties of critic :

(1) Those with something to say and an arresting and lively way of saying it—

(2) Those with nothing to say and an arresting and lively way of saying it—

(3) Those with nothing to say and a dull, vulgar or dead way of saying it.

Sometimes, in the days of my youth, I used to fancy myself rather high up in the second of these categories. But now that I am, like the dramatist in *Present Laughter*, advancing with every sign of reluctance into middle age, I am not at all so sure about myself. (I am far more sure about my colleagues and the categories where *they* belong.)

My own eventual undoing as a critic will be the fatal streak of kindness in me! A good critic has no business to be consciously kind or consciously unkind: it is his sole business to be just and nothing but just, whether to plays or producers or performers. When I explain this in exactly these terms to stage-folk who thank me for having been "kind", they stare, and their gaze is as cold and uncomprehending as the moon's.

ALAN DENT

HAROLD HOBSON

WHAT IS DRAMATIC CRITICISM? Poetry, said Quiller-Couch, is the stuff that poets have written. So I suppose that dramatic criticism is what has been written by dramatic critics. Hazlitt, when he went to the theatre, wrote superbly about the acting he saw there. Bernard Shaw, when he saw a play, wrote magnificently about the sort of play that in his opinion ought to have been acted in preference to the play that he had seen. Max Beerbohm wrote idiosyncratically about himself. All three were excellent critics: which suggests that dramatic criticism is wider in range than it is generally supposed to be.

Nevertheless, I think that one may dare to say that a piece of dramatic criticism to be really acceptable should, in general, contain remarks, on the one hand, about the play the critic has seen and, on the other, about the way the play was acted. The proportions between the two sections of the criticism are subject to almost infinite variation. Sometimes it is the play that gets nearly all the attention. This was often the case with William Archer, who was popularly supposed to end many of his reviews with the remark, "I will write about the acting next week". And sometimes, as with Hazlitt, it is the players who reap the principal harvest of the critic's judgment.

Ideally, of course, the proportions should be governed, not by the critic's personal taste but by the relative value of the writing and the playing. In France to-day, for example, where the most influential workers in the literary world are men who contribute regularly to the theatre, there are many cogent reasons why the critic should devote perhaps the greater part

HAROLD HOBSON

of his talents and time to the correct evaluation of the literary and theatrical worth of the script the author has provided.

In England the situation is rather different. I do not wish to be understood as suggesting for a moment that the British theatre lacks able and exciting authors; at the same time, it is obvious even to the most casual and thoughtless visitor to the West End playhouses that we are living in a period when English acting is at one of the peaks of its achievement. Whenever I go to the theatre I am conscious that there is a possibility that I may be going to have a considerable emotional experience, in which fine acting is likely to play a preponderant part.

Now it may be, it undoubtedly is, useful to evaluate and analyse that experience. But there is something else to be done as well, something which I cannot help feeling is even more important: that is, to take that experience and to record it, and by recording it give it some sort of permanence. This perhaps is not so much the critic's approach to the drama as the historian's; and, if the term were not pompous, I think that dramatic critics might gain a truer view of their functions if they were called, not critics, but historians.

A dramatic critic, then, ought to have an eye for detail. If he has no eye for detail, he will never make a dramatic historian, for it is the detail that gives life. If he cannot distinguish the significant detail from the insignificant, he will be only a gossip-writer. But if he can recreate on the page what he has seen and heard on the stage, and at the same time convey the emotional impression it has made on him, he will, in my opinion, be discharging his functions in a just and honourable manner.

PHILIP HOPE-WALLACE

ACTRESSES, actors and dramatists who in that order live on applause dislike criticism which is not praise (in which case they seldom demur). Do they pay too much attention to criticism? Yes. Yet we are told they never read their "notices". That is as it should be; critics do not write for them but for audiences, which like to have an opinion to set against their own (often very violent). Notice "against".

No one pretends critics are infallible. They differ among themselves—of course; when Mr. Attlee makes a speech, what the *Daily Herald* and *The Times* say next day differs, sometimes greatly. The best critic will be the epitome of the best part of any given audience, its head, heart and soul. He should be the best instructed member of that audience in all matters abstract concerning the drama, in all its departments and manifestations, *provided* he is not a specialist in any one of them. Above all, he should have no special "inside" knowledge of what "they" (behind the footlights) have been up to to produce the effect he is surrendering to.

A critic is concerned with the end product, not with the means of manufacture. You don't have to be an egg to make an omelette; nor a cook to know a good omelette from a bad one; above all, not a personal friend of the cook and in difficulty in tasting his omelette because you know his wife is deceiving him and that the kitchen caught fire earlier in the day. A *gourmet* needs some experience of cooking in different parts of the globe and a reasonably clean palate; but the palate is the important thing. A good palate will determine what the thing is and then whether it is well done or not. The immediate Why will be, at best, a guess.

The audience pays for its seats; the critic does not, as it might prejudice him into thinking he had not had value for money. All criticism is opinion; all opinion is prejudiced. But

PHILIP HOPE-WALLACE

a critic can school himself out of certain sorts of prejudice; as for instance that jealousy which, in my view, often makes failed actors very bad critics of their colleagues' work.

Another distraction is the belief that criticism is an exact science with a set of academic rules by which a critic should allot marks in the manner of an adjudicator. Equally, it is important to avoid being a *laudator temporis acti* for its own sake, or an enthusiast for a thing merely because it is new. A *gourmet* never tires of bread and cheese, but should avoid too many custard pies. (This is not always possible; we live in a wicked world, if Mr. Fry will allow it.)

Undistracted attention may not produce good criticism, but it should produce sincerity. This may lead to inflicting pain, which is unpleasant, like drawing teeth. But in the end a dentist who lies is a villain. If criticism, nowadays much milder than it used to be—some angry galleryites would say it was all too soft—hurts artists, no part of whose duty it is to be thick-skinned, let them not read it; anyhow, their point of view will still be radically different from that of audience and critic. (I do not mean that Mr. Fry's charmingly expressed message falls on deaf ears, because it is delivered with such good nature. *Excelsior*, by all means. But we too have our difficulties.)

Criticism dubbed harlotry in places where it has given offence can (as Mr. Fry's address perhaps shows, though not as much as the writings of, say, G.B.S., Archer or C. E. Montague or Desmond MacCarthy) often be as fully creative an art as that of playmaking or acting. It is of course a different form of creation, as different perhaps as market gardening from cooking or eating from either. Likewise, the writing of history may be as creative as the making of it. Both are an interpretation of Life.

All departments contain duds; and it would be too sanguine, I fear, to hope that after all these centuries every kind of interpreter of Life should see eye to eye. But one can try, now and again; we will try, Mr. Fry.

ERIC KEOWN

ERIC KEOWN

BEING ONE of the few critics who have to scrape the mud off
their boots on first nights, my main approach to dramatic
criticism is the Southern Railway. But I have also been asked
to state my subsidiary lines of approach, and that's not so
easy.

I don't believe that to-day the critic has any profound in-
fluence on the drama of his time. The fear which he inspired
among playwrights and actors towards the end of the nineteenth
century has weakened steadily. The trend of drama is now
dictated much less by expert opinion than by mass taste, in the
formation of which Hollywood, the Light Programme, and the
distorting mirrors of modern publicity play an increasing part.
Unanimous praise by the critics can still fill a theatre for a short
time, but their heaviest broadsides will not diminish the queues
for a celluloid queen or for a farce that has faithfully reached
the knuckle.

There remains, however, a small section of the public that
will take the trouble to read what is underneath the pictures,
and for this the critic acts as a barometer, telling it what sort
of theatrical weather to expect. Like all barometers, he requires
constant adjustment, and it seems to me that his first duty is
to be aware of his own state of mind. I mean that by a conscious
process he must be fair to the kind of play that isn't really his
weight, or to an actor or actress whose personality is out of
tune with his. He must make allowances for spasms of private
joy or gloom unconnected with the play in question (I have
always thought the contents of the reviewer's stomach should
be listed in italics below his article, and more than ever now

that the theatres clash with dinner). He must try to remember that actors have their off-days just as much as bus-drivers or jugglers. And yet at the back of his mind he must contrive to carry an uncorrupted standard of perfection.

Of course there is no science of criticism. We are all bound to have our own slants, and without them critics would be duller than ditchwater. Because of this, I think it is as important for a reader to know his critic, testing him over a period long enough to bring familiarity with his moods and the nature of his pet bees, as it is for the critic to know his theatre.

Not that the critic can be expected to know all about the theatre. I see no reason why he should, for he is not concerned with how things are done but only with their effect on his senses. And about his senses there can be nothing magical. He is simply (he hopes) an intelligent playgoer who has trained himself to absorb impressions as accurately as possible; who, by reading and experience, has acquired certain ideals of taste and developed a background against which he can sort out these impressions and put them into perspective; and who can pass them on coherently.

The job of the weekly critic differs slightly from that of his daily brethren, and not only because they wake next morning with their pronouncements enviably in print. His readers are likely to be spread over a larger area, and therefore fewer will probably ever see the production he is describing. For this reason I think he should take particular pains to make his account as complete in itself as he can.

I haven't mentioned the feeling of innocent excitement as the curtain rises, in whatever theatre, on whatever play. Unless he can preserve this undimmed, the critic would do better to shell peas or go into Parliament.

J. C. TREWIN

WHAT IS MY APPROACH to dramatic criticism? . . . It is not easy to reply without granting oneself, by implication, a First Class (Hons.) degree in the virtues. That must be risked.

I am a dramatic critic because I love the theatre. I prefer to approach it as a friend, seeking the best, than as an enemy with the phrase that withers: another Young Marcius preparing to mammock the gilded butterfly. Few things in journalism (and a critic is a journalist) are simpler than condemnation. "Let the Word thump 'ee with great thumps!" said a preacher in my native village. Often young men begin by thumping; they grow out of it, learn to realise that nothing is more ingenuous than extreme sophistication.

To appreciate, in the best sense, is harder, more rewarding. Enjoy yourself, said C. E. Montague. "To make people like a thing you must delight in it first." But (some argue) should not the critic be the "Keep Out" notice, the growling dog, the speck of ratsbane? I feel that any writer perpetually cynical, perpetually displeased, should find work more congenial. It is possible to keep standards high, to be selective, to do the reader service without being ashamed of a decent courtesy ("softness" is, I fear, the cant phrase) or regretting that a notice has not been inscribed upon asbestos.

I don't think a critic needs to have written a play or to have acted. I do think he should appreciate the niceties of theatrical technique, the dramatist's, the actor's, the producer's. He should be able, during any performance, to separate the strands of which it is made.

Every critic should know the provinces. He cannot afford to have the metropolitan mind which holds that no work of value is done outside the square mile or so of the West End, or the

53

theatres of another capital. The more plays he can hear and read the better. A long memory is useful; he should be proud of the record of the English theatre (not in London alone). A sense of the past is never a handicap.

Let me summarise. Ideally, a critic must be ready and anxious to write about Shakespeare and the Crazy Gang, Ibsen or Stephen Phillips or the little comedy last night. He must not be snobbish. He must approach any play, any performance, expectantly, and always—a detachment that is hard but essential—with a mind unblurred by an author's or a player's reputation. That saves him from the stencil-judgment, from assuming that because an actor has done this or the other in one part he must necessarily do it in the next.

A critic must be a Summoner. He must find words that fit the occasion, get his readers to feel, to hear, to see. He must try, without exhibitionism and without pretending that he is the voice on Sinai, to get something of himself into his notices.

What more? I am asked often whether a critic ought not to be trained formally, to descend upon the theatre properly licensed (or, as one questioner said with the best intentions in the world, "certified"). The answer, very simply, is that a dramatic critic trains himself by going to the theatre. For my part I thank the "Rep" of a western city at which I learned not to despise the late Victorian and Edwardian dramatists, to recognise the cheerful theatrical alarums of melodrama, to be at home with, say, *The Way of the World*, *London Assurance*, *Under Two Flags*, *Mid-Channel*, *Mr. Pim Passes By*, and *Heartbreak House*.

It was the right introduction to the most exciting task in modern letters: the most exciting if, I repeat, a critic comes to the theatre always as a candid (but never a malicious) lover; if he keeps his hope burnished and his eagerness unfrayed.

J. C. TREWIN

T. C. WORSLEY

T. C. WORSLEY

I WAS PRESENT on the occasion when Mr. Christopher Fry addressed the Critics' Circle, and rose several times to speak but failed to catch the Chairman's eye. Had I been lucky enough to do so, I should have tried to spoil the atmosphere of good-will and mutual congratulation which his address generated by saying something like this:

"Mr. Chairman, this is all very well, this bleating of the jackals made up as lambs and this cooing of the serpent im-personating a dove. But it is all part of the grand illusion that brings us together. The critics and the workers in the theatre cannot lie down together; they speak a different language and inhabit a different climate. They both have the same end in view, the good of the theatre. But they approach the thing from such opposite angles that they must be content to appear enemies. Once critics fall into the trap of viewing the theatre with the same eyes as the author or the actor, their usefulness is at an end. They might, by doing so, appear to be more knowledge-able and more generous, but standards would inevitably sink. What authors, actors and producers want is praise. Praise, praise and then more praise. Naturally enough. So do we all. What, on the other hand, they *need*, whether they know it or not, is discrimination. And that is what we are there to supply."

What else does Mr. Fry's plea come down to in the end except this? The age-long cry of the artist and the child: "Love me. Understand me. Praise me." But the good parent must sometimes harden her heart against her child and refuse. If she didn't, the child would never grow up. As to understanding, it is the business of the writer to make himself understood and, if he doesn't—in the theatre above all places—it is the busi-ness of the critic to tell him so. Of course, he may write off the critics as nit-wits and comfort himself with the belief that posterity will understand. Well, I cheerfully give him posterity. But you notice that he isn't content with that. Most of our modern playwrights share something else with the child— the insistence on having it both ways. They want the seventy thousand a year and the chorus of adulation while they live, and the diners, few but choice, when they are dead as well.

This demand for praise from workers in the theatre is not, by the way, just the product of a swollen vanity. On the contrary, it is right; it is essential. Praise and adulation are their natural element; out of it they would gasp and die like fishes out of water. For every theatrical production is a gigantic act of faith and, if everyone didn't spend their time persuading everyone else how marvellous everyone was, how superb the play and brilliant the author, how exciting the production and clever the producer, the show would never get on at all. It is the great shot of self-praise injected into the collective arm that brings them up to the pitch where they believe completely in their fond illusion.

But all this has nothing to do with the critic. He is concerned only with the finished product. And it would be fatal for him to concern himself with anything else. I think this is why theatrical people get such a shock sometimes when, feverishly, they turn to the notices. They are still in a sweat from the stuffy atmosphere of adulation in which they have been living for weeks or months, and the cool air of the critic strikes them as horribly cold.

But we must refuse the temptation of confusing the two functions—those of the critic and the worker in the theatre. The difference between them is best summed up in their respective mottoes. For the motto of theatre people, you must know, is written in fluorescent lighting above every stage dressing-room. It reads—"Darling, you were wonderful!" The motto of the critic is muttered to himself every time he picks up his ill-paid pen—"Don't flatter yourself. Keats died of consumption."

First-Night Scene

WHO'S WHO
among the critics

The eight critics invited to complete this book were chosen because of merit and the amount of space at their disposal. There are many others among those listed on page 63 who have strong claims to be included, but the size of the book was limited.

We particularly deplore the absence of Mr. A. V. Cookman. Unfortunately he writes for a newspaper that believes in anonymity, but his first-night habit of looking, before every curtain rise, as if he expected a miracle is an example to us all.

K. W.

IVOR BROWN. Dramatic critic to *The Observer* since 1919, has written four novels, five books about the theatre and one on political theory, but is most successful and prolific on the subject of the English language. Was chiefly responsible for creation of the Drama Section of the C.E.M.A. Has been a leader-writer for *Manchester Guardian* and was editor of *The Observer* for six years before resigning to devote himself to the theatre and literature. A loyal Scot, holds an LL.D. degree from St. Andrews University and D.Litt. from Aberdeen, and has been known to do a sword dance using a handbag for a sporran. Married to producer Irene Hentschel. Handwrites his notices in the office, needs an expert to decipher them but rarely alters in proof. Tends to be monosyllabic with casual acquaintances but intimates produce many stories of kindness by stealth. Not easily impressed by present French school of dramatics. Has a talent for a pun.

W. A. DARLINGTON. (William Aubrey—known generally, and affectionately, as Bill.) Was schoolmaster, soldier, editor (of *The World*) and humorous writer before he had the opportunity to indulge his great passion for the theatre. Became dramatic critic to the *Daily Telegraph* in 1920 and thirty-two years of first nights have done nothing to dim his enthusiasm. Four years after his début as a critic his play "Alf's Button" began breaking theatrical records. Now talks wistfully of his years of prosperity. Has also written six humorous novels, half-a-dozen books on the theatre and an enchanting book of autobiography. In "I Do What I Like" he described dramatic criticism as a Brotherhood—"a heterogeneous collection of men bound together by one love held in common." Secondary enthusiasms are golf and cricket—now played from the lofty reaches of the Over Forties Club.

ALAN DENT. Dramatic critic to *News Chronicle* since 1945. Born Ayrshire, Scotland, 1905, seventeen years of London dramatic criticism has weakened neither his accent nor his reserve, but has provided him with an expert knowledge of the Cockney tongue. Usually attends first nights alone, and forbears any kind of discussion about the play until his notice is written. Began apprenticeship as secretary and assistant to James Agate in 1926, who bequeathed him his collection of books on the theatre. Became London critic for the *Manchester Guardian* in 1935 and critic for *Punch* in 1942. A frequent broadcaster, and text editor of films of "Henry V" and "Hamlet". Published works include "Preludes and Studies" and "Nocturnes and Rhapsodies".

HAROLD HOBSON. Dramatic critic to *Christian Science Monitor* for twenty years and succeeded James Agate on *Sunday Times* in 1947, a dangerous assignment which he justified by introducing his own highly individual approach. Camouflages his delight in his work under an air of detachment and a disconcerting willingness to listen to other opinions, frequently withholding his own. Typewrites his notices every Friday morning. As a Sunday-paper man, shares with Ivor Brown the advantage of having the last word. Might fairly be described as primarily an actor's critic. Is an ardent Francophile. Published works include "The Devil in Woodford Wells" (novel), "Theatre" (1948) and "Theatre II" (1950).

PHILIP HOPE-WALLACE. Dramatic critic to *Manchester Guardian*, *Time & Tide*, *The Listener*. The youngest of our contributors, he was born in 1911 and began critical operations in 1945. Previously was *The Times* Correspondent and Public Relations Officer to the Air Force. One of the few critics who actively enjoys the first-night spectacle, it is possible to identify him by his amused expression and habit of balancing both chin and hands on top of his inevitable umbrella. Has profound knowledge of music, and his many broadcasts have made his particular blend of affability and culture familiar to a wide public. In spite of occasional thrusts, his criticism has a comprehension and sympathy which makes him an actors' favourite.

ERIC KEOWN. Dramatic critic to *Punch* since 1945, a member of its staff since 1928 and of the Round Table since 1939. Most easily recognised of the critics, can be seen either towering above all-comers in the gangway or collapsed scissorwise in his seat, chin resting gently between his knees. He is six feet six and a half inches tall. Hand-writes his notices the day after the performance, avoids reading colleagues' daily paper notices until he has recorded his own opinion. Affirms he has no memory for faces, but keeps meticulous card index of actors and actresses who have impressed him in minor parts. Urbane, courteous, fond of good food. Other recreations are fishing, sailing, snuff and encouraging snuff-taking amongst his acquaintances. Author of original story of "Ghost Goes West". Frequent broadcaster on The Critics.

J. C. TREWIN. (John Courtenay.) Cornishman, born in 1908, first dramatic criticism was published at age of twenty in *The Western Independent*. To-day he guides the theatre-going of readers of four weekly magazines (see page 63) and is also assistant to Ivor Brown on *The Observer* and broadcast drama critic to *The Listener*. Travels many hundred miles to see local repertory companies and half across London to encourage Little Theatre activities. Writes an average of two books a year; latest include "Stratford Upon Avon", "The Theatre Since 1900" and "Down to the Lion". Theatre habits include the company of wife Wendy (almost as sound and articulate a judge as himself); wearing coat and muffler throughout the year, and a tray of coffee in first interval. Has bulging pockets, enormous tolerance and the ability to write a thoughtful notice of one play while he sits listening to another.

T. C. WORSLEY. Dramatic critic to *The New Statesman & Nation* since 1938. Born 1907, previously a schoolmaster and member of Royal Air Force. Something of a lone wolf in the theatre. Dislikes personal publicity. Has large following among youthful intellectuals. Recently published "Shakespeare's Histories at Stratford" with Dover Wilson, and a collection of criticisms called "The Fugitive Art".

LONDON DRAMATIC CRITICS

JOHN BARBER	*Daily Express*
BEVERLEY BAXTER	*Sunday Express*
IVOR BROWN	*The Observer*
HAROLD CONWAY	*Evening Standard*
A. V. COOKMAN	*The Times*
	Tatler & Bystander
W. A. DARLINGTON	*Daily Telegraph*
	New York Times
ALAN DENT	*News Chronicle*
RICHARD FINDLATER	*The Tribune*
PETER FLEMING	*The Spectator*
ELIZABETH FRANK	*News Chronicle* (2)
R. P. M. GIBBS	*Daily Telegraph* (2)
LOGAN GOURLAY	*Sunday Express*
WALTER HAYES	*Daily Graphic*
HAROLD HOBSON	*Sunday Times*
	Christian Science Monitor
PHILIP HOPE-WALLACE	*Manchester Guardian*
	Time & Tide
FRANK JACKSON	*Reynolds News*
SIRIOL HUGH JONES	*Vogue*
ERIC KEOWN	*Punch*
J. W. LAMBERT	*Sunday Times* (2)
DAVID LEWIN	*Daily Express* (2)
RALPH E. LOVELESS	*The Stage*
P. L. MANNOCK	*Daily Herald*
ROBERT OTTOWAY	*Sunday Graphic*
MOORE RAYMOND	*Sunday Dispatch*
DICK RICHARDS	*Sunday Pictorial*
S. ROSSITER-SHEPHERD	*The People*
J. C. TREWIN	*The Observer* (2)
	John o' London's Weekly
	Illustrated London News
	The Sketch; The Lady
KENNETH TYNAN	*Evening Standard*
STEPHEN WILLIAMS	*Evening News*
A. E. WILSON	*The Star*
CECIL WILSON	*Daily Mail*
T. C. WORSLEY	*New Statesman & Nation*

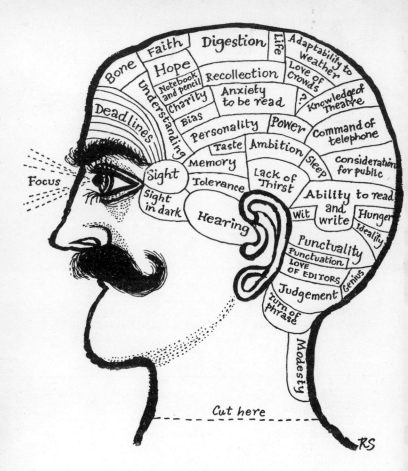

Have you the makings of a
Dramatic Critic?

CHECK YOURSELF AGAINST THIS CHART